TERRY RILEY

THE PIANO WORKS

CHESTER MUSIC

Published by:
Chester Music Limited,

Exclusive distributors:
Hal Leonard
7777 West Bluemound Road,
Milwaukee, WI 53213
Email: info@halleonard.com

Hal Leonard Europe Limited
42 Wigmore Street Maryleborne,
London, WIU 2 RY
Email: info@halleonardeurope.com

Hal Leonard Australia Pty. Ltd.
4 Lentara Court Cheltenham,
Victoria, 9132 Australia
Email: info@halleonard.com.au

Order No. CH83237
ISBN 978-1-78305-864-8
This book © Copyright 2015 by Chester Music.

Edited by Sam Lung.
Music engraved and processed by Elius Gravure Musicale.
Introductory notes by Terry Riley and Sarah Cahill.
Cover designed by Fresh Lemon.
Photo page 4 by Chris Felver/Getty Images.
Photo page 11 by Stuart Brinin.

With special thanks to everybody at G. Schirmer.

CONTENTS

FROM THE COMPOSER

This story starts down on Mrs. Halton's chicken farm on the back road from Colfax to Weimar, California during WWII.

My mother and I were living with my grandparents in the beautiful Sierra Nevada foothills while my father, a US Marine, was off fighting the Japanese in the Pacific for 3 years.

Each Saturday my Italian Nona would drive me to my piano lesson in her 1934 black Plymouth sedan. I would have the lesson (find out where middle C was, etc.) and then she would drive home, me in the back seat with two or three live chickens that were to be magically transformed into Sunday's meal. My Nona, Ida Ridolfi, sang opera in the kitchen while she prepared the most savorous Italian meals imaginable. Every Sunday, unannounced, 20 to 25 guests would come to Weimar, drawn to her legendary feasts. She never knew who exactly would be showing up, but show up they invariably did. She did this ritual joyously all the years I knew her and I might add it was quite a miracle on my Nono's meager salary as a section foreman for the Southern Pacific Railroad. I credit her with being my first Guru and her independent spirit, her generosity, her teachings and example have guided me all these years.

The Southern Pacific Railway trains rolled by 75ft from the small cottage where my Nona and Ma managed to install an old upright piano upon which I began to learn.

I had a cousin named 'Dickie' who could play almost anything he heard on the radio. He would extemporize for hours on popular classic themes, all by ear, never learning to read music. He would also give them fanciful new names. Brahms' Hungarian Dance No. 5 he renamed 'Streffanacci'. I learned to ape all his creations. I also followed his example of learning tunes off the radio by ear, coming as close as I could to what I thought I was hearing. Meanwhile the lessons progressed but 'making stuff up' became my main passion.

After the war, my dad came home and we relocated to Redding, California. By that time, I was starting to learn the classical literature with my new teacher, Mrs. McGorvin and I became the pianist for a small performance group called Grand Dad's Copycats, the brain child of a wonderful man, Walter Ray. It was a kind of Vaudeville show put on by kids and we toured around Northern California playing for Granges and Rotary Clubs and anyone else who would watch and listen. I had an act together with a drummer called Tin

Pan Alley playing tunes like 'Dark Town Strutters Ball'. I really loved playing pieces that were driven by left hand ostinato like the 'Bumble Boogie' and 'Along the Navaho Trail'. Still do!

Redding was a logging town of 10,000 then and very rough around the edges. Walter Ray's group gave kids the opportunity to act, sing, dance and juggle. At the time the Copycats were one of the few cultural outlets available. While in high school two very important teachers turned up in my life: pianist Duane Hampton and violinist/choir director Ralph Wadsworth. They both saw me as raw talent and a sponge eager to soak up all they had to offer. Duane, recently graduated from the Curtis Institute, was a marvelous pianist with an elegant touch. The way his fingers sunk in to the keys using just the weight of his arms impressed me a lot. He played from a place of stillness. Being a frail man, he coaxed rather than pounded but when necessary he could produce sonorities of great power and drama.

Wadsworth discovered that I had perfect pitch and could identify notes and chords without seeing the keys. Alas, somewhere along the way this ability deserted me. Ralph and I spent countless hours outside of class going through his giant record collection. During this period, I was introduced to most of the great 20th century composers. But mainly I would listen over and over to certain works, for instance Bartok's *Music for Strings, Percussion and Celeste* and Poulenc's *Concerto for Two Pianos*. My first composition, 'Evening', was a tune I contributed for a musical Ralph wrote for Shasta High school students where he was an award-winning choir director.

Duane Hampton introduced me to the great Austrian pianist Adolf Baller and I moved to San Francisco to study and begin composition lessons at San Francisco State.

Adolf Baller, an Austrian Jew, had had his hands smashed by the Nazis and after countless surgeries he returned to play chamber music with the Alma Trio from Palo Alto. Baller was one of the warmest human beings I had ever met and a master teacher. His own playing was liquid and warm and his broken hands had mended giving him a strong secure touch. I doubt that he was ever without pain but his smile could warm the most icy heart. He mostly taught the works of Beethoven and Bartok and probably sensed that I would end up in composition. A few years later, working at a United Airlines ticket counter at San Francisco International Airport, I looked up and there was Baller with his luggage. I hadn't seen him or had a lesson in years. It was the last time we were to meet, but his teachings left a lasting imprint on my piano playing.

The *Two Pieces for Piano* (1958/59) were begun while I was working at United Airlines, writing music on my off time. Also I had just gotten married and we had a daughter on the way.

I had begun to play lots of Schoenberg and some intricate Schoenberg-like pieces by composer Loren Rush. I had begun to transition from my Neoclassical period under the spell of Francis Poulenc and Darius Milhaud. The discovery of Schoenberg excited me both as a piano player and composer. I absorbed the rhythmic, textural and melodic angularity of the style without the desire to apply twelve-tone technique to my writing. They were written at the piano a phrase at a time, which I played over and over, modifying the rhythms and pitches until it felt and sounded 'right'.

In the meantime, I went to UC Berkeley and earned a Master's degree in composition. What a composition class! La Monte Young, Loren Rush, David del Tredici, Pauline Oliveros, Douglas Leedy and Jules Langert... with William Denny and Seymour Shifrin presiding. Everyone brought in new and exciting work. It was a prolific bunch of young mavericks, with an array of music ideologies.

With an MA degree in hand, I purchased a hundred dollar ancient jalopy and drove with my wife Ann and three-year-old daughter Colleen from California to New York. There we boarded the SS Saturnia crossing a stormy winter Atlantic to Gibraltar; thus begun a two-year period of living in Europe. I ended up getting a job playing in Fred Payne's Artist Bar in Paris's Pigalle district just up the street from where Olivier Messiaen was playing organ at Trinite. I played all night sessions, happy for the chance to have a piano where I could improvise... the inebriated customers never seeming to notice me. Fred told me Cole Porter had played the same piano in this same bar when he lived in Paris. Down the street at the Eglise de la Sainte-Trinité, Olivier Messiaen played the organ on Sundays.

One night at Fred's, an agent booking floor shows for the Strategic Air Command (SAC) walked in and hired me as a piano accompanist. My job consisted of driving (sometimes for many hours) the artists to the SAC bases, playing piano for the shows and then driving the long way back to Paris. Grueling. But then President Kennedy was assassinated and the SAC bases ceased all entertainment. My job ended. After two years it was

time to head home. But before doing so, I collaborated with playwright Ken Dewey and jazz trumpeter Chet Baker on a Theater of Nations production of Ken's play, *The Gift*. It was through the process working with Baker and developing loops of his playing that I was led to repetitive cells of melody and rhythm that led me later on to the creation of *IN C*.

Our little family returned by passenger liner back to San Francisco in 1964 in time to see my father for a few months before he died. I got my old job back at the Gold Street Saloon where I had worked nights while going to graduate school. Wally Rose, who had played Dixieland with the Turk Murphy band, was still at Gold Street. I owe Wally for generously sharing his knowledge of ragtime. I never really wanted to learn all the rags but I did want to know the secrets of its magic peace-giving grooves and Wally showed me that.

I was asked by friends, Ramon Sender and Morton Subotnick, to give a one-man show at the San Francisco Tape Music Center on Divisadero Street in November of 1964. This was to be the first all-Riley concert and I had been slowly collecting materials for it, including *IN C*, which was premiered on that evening along with many newly-composed tape loop pieces. On the program that night the only piano piece was *Coule*, which later became Keyboard Study No. 1.

I had been playing Keyboard Studies No. 1 and No. 2 (1965) for a couple of years before notating them. Both were repetitive studies of time, hand coordination, improvisational flow and texture. John Cage had asked me for a page of music for his *Notations* book and I submitted Keyboard Study No. 2. These studies are intended to be played as long meditational exercises. Changes over long durations are important to their effect.

Keyboard Study No. 1 is an alternating hand exercise where the pattern of each hand substitutes various notes of the right and left hand cells while keeping up the obsessive alternating rhythm. Keyboard Study No. 2 originated with the basic cell A♭-G-B♭-F and its transposition E♭-D-F-C. It is played first in one hand and then combined with itself with two hands in varying alignments. The basic melodic contour of this four note cell is retained as it also appears in 3, 5, 6, 7, 8, 9, 10, 11 and 12-note patterns; all of which can be combined in any imaginable way. The object is to do this spontaneously in a musical way and to develop a polymetric flow with each hand retaining its independence.

After the Keyboard Studies, my next big piano project was *The Harp Of New Albion* (1983). Dedicated to my lifelong friend La Monte Young and inspired by his Well Tuned Piano, this multi-sectioned, two-hour work was created for a five-limit system in just intonation. Each movement is a long raga-like improvisation based on various structural ideas that have a different definition for each section. *The New Albion Chorale* is the only section that has been notated. It was transcribed by Toon Vandevorst using my notes and the *Celestial Harmonies* recording.

At a few points in my life, my work has intersected with the 1960's British Rock scene. It has gone both ways. I had jams with Daevid Allen and the Soft Machine when they were just starting out. Pete Townshend honored me with The Who's great tune, *Baba O'Riley*. *The Walrus In Memoriam* (1983) came about at the instigation of pianist Aki Takahashi for her Hyper Beatles project with Beatles tunes arranged for her by various composers.

The Heaven Ladder, Book 7 was commissioned in 1994. These five pieces have the distinction of being my first set of through-composed piano works since the 1959 *Two Pieces for Piano*. A 35-year gap!

The bookends for the collection are *Misha's Bear Dance* and *Simone's Lullaby*. Misha and Simone are my daughter Colleen's twin grandchildren born also in 1994.

Simone's Lullaby was intended to be looped and played all during the night for the sleeping twins. At the last measure it says 'Repeat until sleeping' and it was my intention that some pianists take this seriously and perform it live until the audience all fall asleep.

Venus In '94 is a somewhat sensuous and romantic propulsive waltz with echoes of Ravel.

Ragtempus Fugatis is a bow to my life as a student writing fugues by day and playing ragtime by night.

Fandango On The Heaven Ladder... well, who doesn't love the grace of a fandango, this one set off and interlaced with poignant chorale sections.

It must be pointed out here that the periods of my musical activity are only occasionally punctuated by notated scores. All during the 70s I toured extensively giving long durational concerts on electric organs tuned in just intonation. This was a form that paralleled my studies and understanding of the long exposition and melodic and rhythmic development of North Indian raga. These forms defy notation. They resist being put into any container but have a boundless passion to emulate the Sound Current which is free in its eternal responsibility of holding the Universe together. To this day, this is the way I like to operate musically. But as a by-product, these notated pieces are like pages from a diary, a sort of 'fallen petals along the way'.

As with many other of my piano works, *Be Kind To One Another (Rag)* (2008–2014) began as a late night improvisation. Its old-timey ragtime references and somewhat naïve and at times romantic atmosphere hooked me from the beginning, and it soon became a late night hit with the grandchildren. In its improvised version, it is basically laid out in six related sections (A, B, C, D, E and F). Each section can take many forms with each section being repeated and extemporized upon as many times as desired before moving on to the next. When the last section is concluded it can jump back to any one of the first three sections and from there create different variations on each section until ending usually on section B. When Sarah Cahill told me about her *Sweeter Music* project, I decided to contribute this work and to make a through-composed concert version, somewhat more virtuosic and grander than the original improvisation. I gave the material a more overall long-arching structure and I added related interludes and developments that were not in the improvisations. The title is taken from something Alice Walker said at a gathering, which took place in the days immediately following 9/11 as she was introducing the eminent Vietnamese Buddhist teacher Thich Nhat Hanh. Her words struck me as the most profound response of all coming out of that calamity.

*"We must learn to
be kind to one another now."*

YES. We must!

Terry Riley
March 2015

PERFORMANCE NOTES

As one of America's most brilliant and innovative virtuoso composer-pianists, Terry Riley has written (and is writing!) a body of piano music which is extremely satisfying to play and immediately appealing to audiences. The best way to approach any of the scores in this volume is to listen to Riley at the piano. Hearing him in concert is best, but recordings are good as well, and there are some terrific videos available online, for instance his Moscow Conservatory recital from 2000. Listen to his *Lisbon Concert* album (New Albion Records) to get a feel for his strong left hand — how it's often equally balanced with his right hand — and his sparse use of pedal, how he accents particular chords, and his quicksilver shifts of mood and style. But Riley's piano music is also open to a variety of interpretations. He himself says "I actually look forward to being surprised by the approaches different pianists will have to these pieces."

It's also helpful to know who his inspirations have been. Listen to the stride piano playing of James P. Johnson and Willie 'The Lion' Smith, the jazz piano of Art Tatum, Erroll Garner, Bud Powell and Bill Evans; also listen to North Indian raga and to Riley's early keyboard masterpieces like *A Rainbow In Curved Air* and *Shri Camel*. Because this collection spans Riley's entire career, from the 1965 Keyboard Studies to the present day, the pianist will be challenged by a wide range of styles. Interestingly, though, Riley is not an eclectic composer. He never dabbles; the shifting genres in his work are woven into its structural integrity. Like Walt Whitman, he might say: "Do I contradict myself? Very well, then I contradict myself, I am large, I contain multitudes." *Fandango on the Heaven Ladder*, *The Walrus In Memorium*, *Ragtempus Fugatis* and *Be Kind To One Another (Rag)* are epic works especially brimming with those multitudes.

TWO PIECES FOR PIANO

Composed when Riley was a student at U.C. Berkeley, studying the rigors of dodecaphonism, these pieces clearly require a radically different approach from the others in this volume. He uses a Schoenbergian precision with regards to dynamic markings, rests, accents, and accelerandos and ritardandos. All this needs to be followed with extreme care. But at the same time, the young Riley can't resist a delicious bluesy chord (Piece No. 2, measures 40–42) or a bit of a jazzy arpeggio (Piece No. 2, measure 72), and these should be enjoyed in performance. And what does one do with the marking '*almost* **mf**' in measure 9 of Piece No. 1? While Riley had yet to find his distinctive compositional voice, these are clearly the work of a composer destined to write for the piano.

KEYBOARD STUDIES

Riley says he first scored the Keyboard Studies at the request of John Cage, for inclusion in *Notations*, a collection of graphic scores from various composers, and wasn't necessarily thinking of performance. The best approach to the Keyboard Studies is to do what Riley himself has done over the years: to use them as a kind of morning meditation exercise. Slowly combine two figures and get comfortable with them, until you feel you're in a groove, and then change the figure in your right or left hand, paying attention to the interlocking patterns which emerge. This technique doesn't come naturally to classically trained pianists, so it's important to give it time and patience, and gradually work up to a faster speed. The Keyboard Studies also provide excellent preparation for any minimalist or postminimalist piano music. The hands should be independent and equally balanced. A piano with a responsive action is required for the rapid repeated notes when two figures collide. The duration of a Keyboard Study is up to the performer.

MISHA'S BEAR DANCE

Playing *Misha's Bear Dance*, one can understand why Riley was celebrated in Russia when he travelled there in 2000; the Russian journal *Izvestia* hailed him as 'the great composer-pianist since Prokofiev'. Certainly there are echoes here of the last movement of Prokofiev's Seventh Sonata, which shares the meter of 7/8. It's important to get a sense of swing in the irregular meters, and again, a strong left hand is essential. In his improvisations, Riley is constantly developing material almost imperceptibly, so the entire atmosphere of a piece transforms around one constant riff. This is also one of his trademark techniques as a composer. Starting at measure 24, he sets up a figure of alternating fourths in the right hand — and it must be rhythmically exact — accompanied by a tender lyrical tune which emerges out of the opening angular bass line. He then transfers the alternating fourths to the left hand while the right embarks on brilliant virtuosic passagework, and soon the figure returns to the right hand while the left starts a minimalist figure. That riff of fourths and fifths must anchor the entire piece, whatever else is in motion around it.

VENUS IN 94

One of the challenges here is to create a lilting waltz and still maintain an inexorable sense of momentum. Even though the right hand has most of the figurations, a strong left hand is required for anchoring the rhythm. Pay special attention to the phrase markings of varying lengths. Dynamic markings are fairly sparse, but the melodic line should be shaped, sometimes voluptuously and sometimes subtly, and at no point should the music be all one static dynamic level simply because a passage is marked *piano*. In measures 173–176, Riley interjects the B-A-C-H motif, but the reference may have been written on a subconscious level.

RAGTEMPUS FUGATIS

Ragtempus Fugatis is probably the most technically difficult piece in this volume, because of its long sustained chromatic passages with strings of thirds and sixths, because of its dense counterpoint traversing multiple key changes, and because of the stamina and bravura required to sustain the toccata-like drive, in perpetual motion up to the last page **fff** finale full of double octaves and finger-busting chords. The fusion of ragtime and fugue is yet another example of the unlikely but brilliant convergences in Riley's piano music, and this too has its challenges. The pianist needs a sense of playfulness throughout this bravura showpiece. In her recording, Gloria Cheng swings the right hand sixteenth notes in measures 12–16, and whenever the ragtime theme occurs thereafter. Careful pacing is crucial, to build towards the final climax.

FANDANGO ON THE HEAVEN LADDER

Most important in performing this vibrant piece is to maintain continuity and structural integrity through its many contrasting sections. The opening chords (which can be voiced in numerous ways) contain the kernel which generates the entire *Fandango*, so the pianist should convey how the seemingly disconnected sections are bound together by harmonic underpinnings. The extroverted *Fandango* theme morphs into a slinky *pianissimo* melody at measure 63 and again at measure 142, and the opening harmonic progression returns with a funky groove at measure 163. The 32nd note mordents exchanged between hands from measures 107–123 should be crisp and clear, like an uninterrupted dialogue. Classical pianists will especially enjoy what seems to be a quote from the last movement of Beethoven's 'Tempest' Sonata in the last three measures.

SIMONE'S LULLABY

Riley's original version of this piece has an indication to 'keep the soft pedal down throughout', and even if it's not used, this should be the effect. The pianist should find fingerings which enable a legato line, beginning with the opening chords. Some damper pedal will need to be used, even if it's not marked — for instance during the left hand leaps in measures 48–54. The arc of the opening four-bar phrase carries through the entire piece, and in addition there's the interplay between the left hand and right hand melodies, which are rarely aligned but should be equally delineated. The note at the end of this lullaby for Riley's granddaughter is 'Repeat until sleeping', but this might not work in the context of a concert performance.

THE WALRUS IN MEMORIUM

For this piece, the pianist should be familiar enough with The Beatles' song 'I Am The Walrus' to recognize that almost every measure here contains a fragment of the song, although the unsettling psychedelia is disguised as a jaunty rag. As with other pieces in this collection, *Walrus* travels through an ever-shifting landscape of styles and moods, from the opening swinging rag to the tender lyricism of the "Sitting in an English garden" quote at measure 62 to the minimalist patterns which follow, tracing the repeated pitches of "I am the eggman, I am the walrus". Riley also conjures up the song's complex orchestration, the melody's dotted rhythms, and the lovely blue-note descending figure of "I'm crying". In the last three pages, reminiscent of Bach's C minor Prelude from the *Well-Tempered Clavier*, the hands travel further and further apart until they're at the extremes of register, the right hand venturing into the stratospheric range which concludes the Beatles' song, while the left hand descends into the lowest bass.

BE KIND TO ONE ANOTHER (RAG)

Like many of Riley's piano works, *Be Kind To One Another* evolved out of material he had improvised over the years, honing various riffs and passagework to crystallize into a fully-formed composition. When his grandchildren Simone and Misha were little, they would ask Riley to play this music as a kind of lullaby, which should be taken into account when interpreting this piece: its gentle nature should carry through, starting with the opening. Here it is helpful to listen to Riley's own playing of 4/4 minimalist patterns, in which he always creates a melody to subvert the beat — in the opening measures, for instance, bringing out the top E and F and phrasing a clear melodic line. The left hand bass should be very present when it enters at measure 9. The entire piece is in 4/4, but the pianist should experiment with accents and flexible phrasing to avoid the regularity of four beats. Riley has revised this piece a few times over the years, filling out the harmonies and adjusting variations here and there, just as he would in improvised versions. Again, the pianist needs to be prepared to negotiate minimalism, jazz, ragtime, stride piano and swinging 16ths all in one piece.

THE PHILOSOPHER'S HAND

The main challenge in this piece is to infuse it with the spontaneity of Riley's improvisation, from which it was faithfully transcribed by Toon Vandervorst. It's helpful to listen to Riley's recording of it (on *Requiem For Adam*, Nonesuch Records) and become familiar with his inflections, his hesitations, his marvelous shadowy tone in the opening and conclusion, and the way he uses grace notes as subtle accents. The bass C-G-D chord grounds the piece throughout, so that should be very present. A performance should have an exploratory quality, with the fermatas providing some suspense, and a flexible, free melodic line.

Sarah Cahill
March 2015

Commissioned by Sarah Cahill for her 'A Sweeter Music' project

BE KIND TO ONE ANOTHER (RAG)

TERRY RILEY
2008, revised 2014

A little slower

A tempo

poco rit.

Commissioned by Kathleen Supove, Gloria Cheng and Stephen Drury

MISHA'S BEAR DANCE

No.1 from *THE HEAVEN LADDER BOOK 7*

TERRY RILEY
1994

Commissioned by Kathleen Supove, Gloria Cheng and Stephen Drury

VENUS IN 94

No.2 from *THE HEAVEN LADDER BOOK 7*

TERRY RILEY
1994

Commissioned by Kathleen Supove, Gloria Cheng and Stephen Drury

RAGTEMPUS FUGATIS

No.3 from *THE HEAVEN LADDER BOOK 7*

TERRY RILEY
1994

45

Commissioned by Kathleen Supove, Gloria Cheng and Stephen Drury

FANDANGO ON THE HEAVEN LADDER
No.4 from *THE HEAVEN LADDER BOOK 7*

TERRY RILEY
1994

Commissioned by Kathleen Supove, Gloria Cheng and Stephen Drury

SIMONE'S LULLABY

No.5 from *THE HEAVEN LADDER BOOK 7*

TERRY RILEY
1994

KEYBOARD STUDY No. 1

PERFORMANCE DIRECTIONS

∞ = A repeating figure

∞∞∞ = A continuum figure

The two kinds of figures interlock and are repeated in this fashion until one of the hands selects another figure.

THE TEMPO IS AS FAST AS CAN BE COMFORTABLY PLAYED.

1. Combine any figure from lines 2–6 with continuum figure 1.

2. If any figure from lines 2–6 is placed in the alignment of continuum figure 1 (beginning with 𝄿 ♪) it may be combined with other figures from lines 2–6.

3. Combine any figure from lines 8–10 with continuum figure 7.

4. If any figure from lines 8–10 is placed in the alignment of continuum figure 7 (beginning with 𝄿 ♪) it may be combined with other figures from lines 8–10.

5. Combine any figure from lines 8–10 with continuum figure 1.

6. If any figure from lines 2–6 is placed in the alignment of continuum figure 1 (beginning with 𝄿 ♪) it may be combined with other figures from lines 8–10.

7. Combine any figure from lines 12–16 with continuum figure 7.

8. Combine any figure from lines 12–16 with continuum figure 11.

9. If any figure from lines 12–16 is placed in the alignment of continuum figure 11 (beginning with 𝄿 ♪) it may be combined with other figures from lines 12–16.

10. Combine any figure from lines 8–10 with continuum figure 11.

11. If any figure from lines 2–6 is placed in the alignment of continuum figure 11 (beginning with 𝄿 ♪) it may be combined with other figures from lines 12–16.

12. If any figure from lines 8–10 is placed in the alignment of continuum figure 11 (beginning with 𝄿 ♪) it may be combined with other figures from lines 12–16.

13. If continuum figure 1 is placed in alignment of figure 2 (beginning with 𝄿 ♪) it may be played against continuum figures 7 or 11.

14. If continuum figure 8 is placed in alignment of figure 9 (beginning with 𝄿 ♪) it may be combined with continuum figures 1 or 11.

KEYBOARD STUDY No. 1

TERRY RILEY
1965

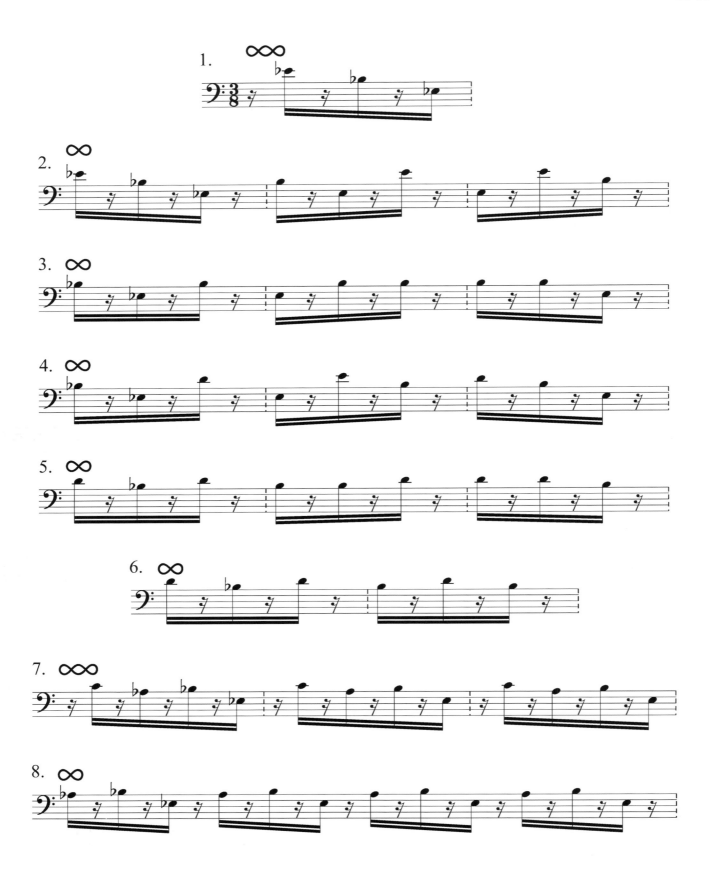

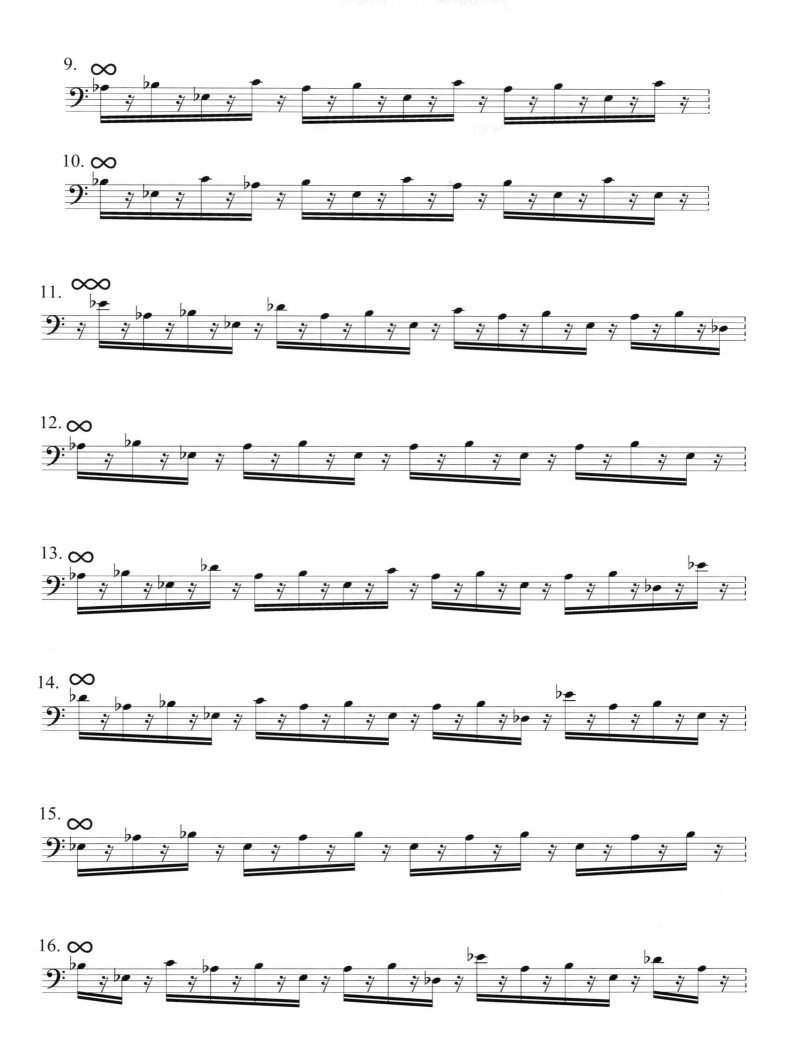

KEYBOARD STUDY No. 2

PERFORMANCE DIRECTIONS

Each cell is represented by a series of note heads. All note heads in the series are of equal value but any cell can be played in augmentation or diminution as well.

Cells can be repeated any number of times; most successfully if the cell unit durations last many minutes.

Each cell can be played in the octave written or transposed up or down by octaves.

Each cell can begin on any note head of the cells

Each cell can be played alone or in combination with itself or any other cell.

A performance may consist of cells from column one only or cells from column two only or a combination of cells from both columns.

The Persian Surgery Dervish cells (a), (b) and (c) can be played as a prelude to Keyboard Study No.2.

The 5 unit cell (a) is played 3 units in the time of 2 units 3:2 of cell (c).

The 10 unit cell (b) is played 3 units in the time of 2 units 3:2 of cell (c).

Cells (a) and (b) can be played against themselves during interludes when cell (c) is not present.

Cell (c) can be played against itself an octave apart. The right hand in diminution values 2:1 and 3:2.

KEYBOARD STUDY No. 2

TERRY RILEY
1965, revised 2015

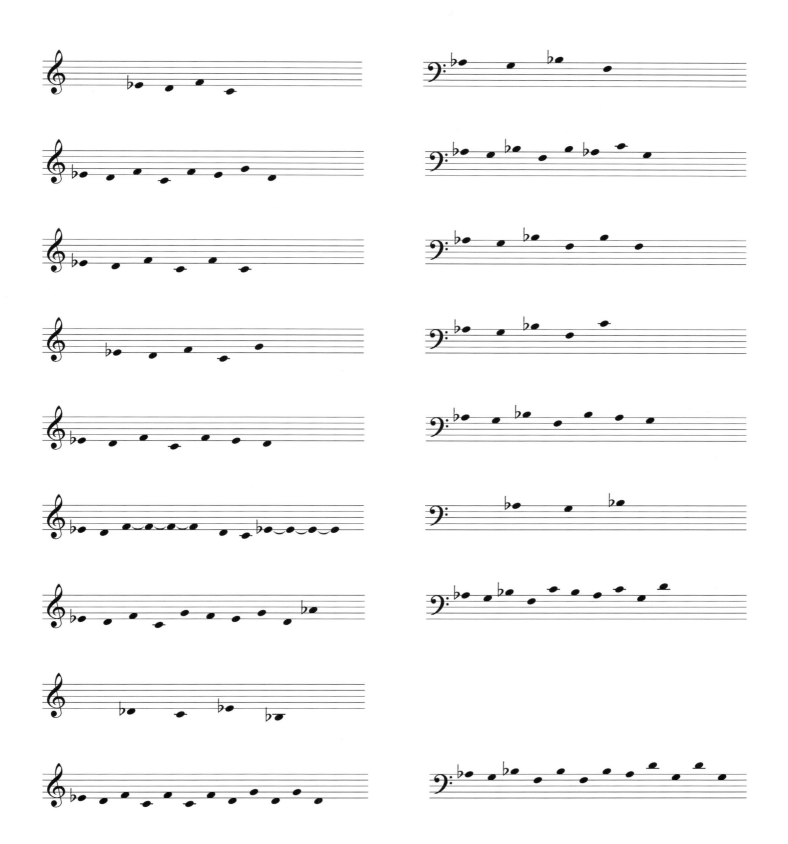

TWO PIECES FOR PIANO

No. I

TERRY RILEY
1958/59

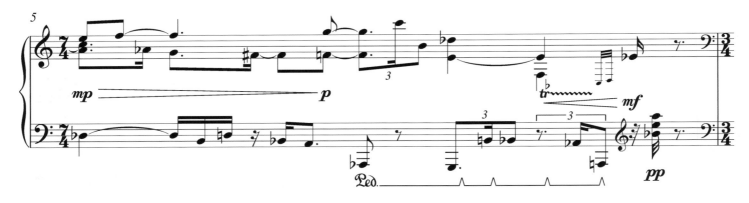

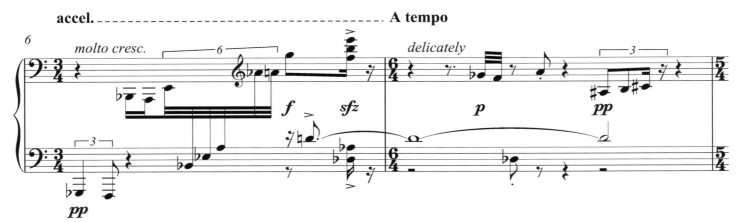

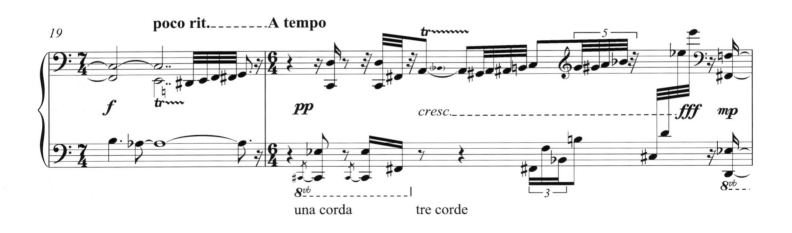

TWO PIECES FOR PIANO

No. 2

TERRY RILEY
1958/59

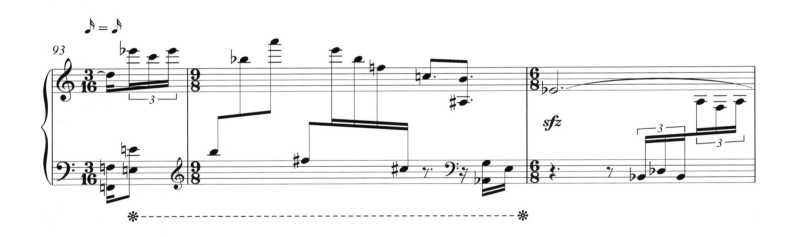

THE PHILOSOPHER'S HAND

TERRY RILEY
2000
TRANSCRIBED BY TOON VANDEVORST

Commissioned by Aki Takahashi for her Hyper Beatles project

THE WALRUS IN MEMORIAM

TERRY RILEY
1993

Straight ♪s

bell-like, build resonance

℘ed. down until m.138

Keyboard Study No. 2 in its circular form
(page 8 of Terry Riley's hand-drawn circular scores)

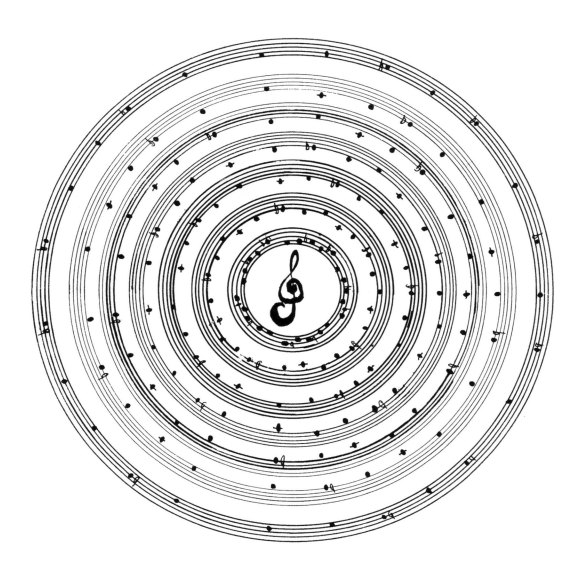

ORIGINAL MANUSCRIPTS

The following facsimiles are of some original manuscripts by the composer, some of which were revised and reconceived for this collection.

KEYBOARD STUDY No. 1 (1965)

RE-COPIED 2005

KeyBOARD
STUDY
#1

Terry Riley

Re. copied by Terry Riley   12 XII 05

KEYBOARD STUDY No. 2 (1965)

RE-COPIED 2005

KEYBOARD STUDY No. 2

50TH ANNIVERSARY REVISION (2015)

TWO PIECES FOR PIANO (1958/59)

FIRST PAGE OF PIECE No. 1